BRYAN ROBSON'S
SOCCER ANNUAL
1989

Mercantile
Credit

Edited by
TOM TYRRELL

HAMLYN

Published in Great Britain in 1988 by
The Hamlyn Publishing Group Limited
a division of The Octopus Publishing Group
Michelin House, 81 Fulham Road
London SW3 6RB
and distributed for them by
Octopus Distribution Services Limited
Rushden, Northamptonshire NN10 9RZ

Copyright © The Hamlyn Publishing
Group Limited 1988

ISBN 0 600 55884 3

Printed in Great Britain

Photographic acknowledgments

Front jacket: top left (Wimbledon) Colorsport; top right (John Barnes) Colorsport; centre (Bryan Robson) All Sport; bottom left (Nigel Clough) All Sport/Simon Bruty; bottom right (Gary Lineker) Colorsport.

Back jacket: top left (Mirandinha) All Sport/Pascal Rondeau; top right (Kenny Dalglish) All Sport; centre (Bryan Robson) All Sport; bottom left (Luton Town) All Sport/Simon Bruty; bottom right (Paul Gascoigne) All Sport/Simon Bruty.

Action Images 42-43; All Sport 11 top, 12, 13 bottom, 41 right, 51 centre left, 55 left, 57 right, (Simon Bruty) 8 right, 18 bottom, 27 top left, 30-31, 35 left, 51 top, (David Cannon) 6, 9 left, 18-19, 21 bottom left, 32, 33 top left, 37 top, 44, 47, 48 left, 56 left, 57 left, 59 left, (Russell Cheyne) 23 bottom right, 45 right, 49 right, (Michael King) 56 right, (Pascal Rondeau) 2-3, 28, (Dan Smith) 15 bottom, 31 right, 36, 62-63, (Billy Stickland) 15 top, 54 right; Colorsport 8 left, 9 right, 10 left and right, 11 bottom, 16 bottom, 17, 20 right, 21 bottom right (inset), 24, 25 top left and right, 27 bottom, 29 top and bottom, 33 right, 34, 39 left, 45 left, 51 bottom, 52, 54 centre, 59 right, 60 left and right; The Daily Telegraph Colour Library 58 top left; Manchester City Football Club 38, 39 right; Doug Poole (London) 37 bottom; Raymonds Photographers (Derby) 26; Sporting Pictures 27 top right, 35 top right, 40, 46, 48-49, 51 centre right, 53 top and bottom, 54 left, 55 centre, 61; Bob Thomas Sports Photography 4-5, 13 top, 14 top and bottom, 16 top, 18 top left and right, 20 top left, 22-23, 23 top, 25 bottom, 41 left, 55 right.

CONTENTS

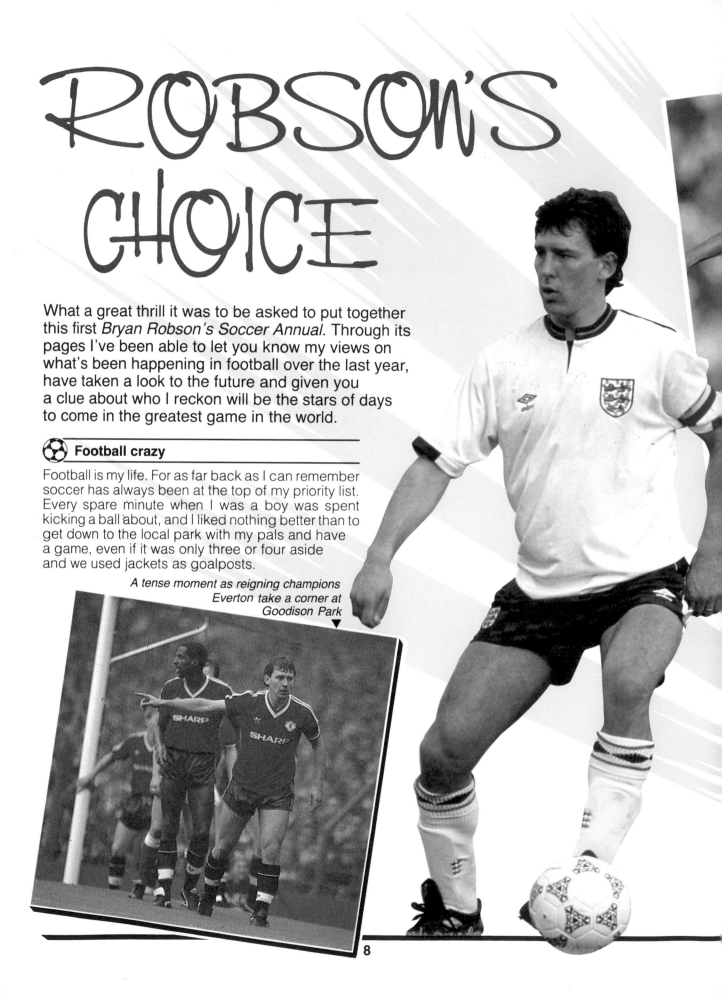

ROBSON'S CHOICE

What a great thrill it was to be asked to put together this first *Bryan Robson's Soccer Annual.* Through its pages I've been able to let you know my views on what's been happening in football over the last year, have taken a look to the future and given you a clue about who I reckon will be the stars of days to come in the greatest game in the world.

⚽ Football crazy

Football is my life. For as far back as I can remember soccer has always been at the top of my priority list. Every spare minute when I was a boy was spent kicking a ball about, and I liked nothing better than to get down to the local park with my pals and have a game, even if it was only three or four aside and we used jackets as goalposts.

A tense moment as reigning champions Everton take a corner at Goodison Park
▼

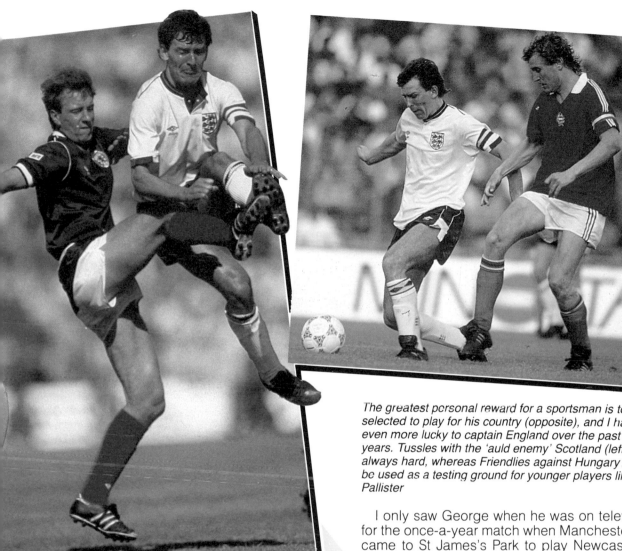

The greatest personal reward for a sportsman is to be selected to play for his country (opposite), and I have been even more lucky to captain England over the past few years. Tussles with the 'auld enemy' Scotland (left) are always hard, whereas Friendlies against Hungary (above) can be used as a testing ground for younger players like Gary Pallister

Does that sound familiar? Are you football crazy too? Well, who knows, perhaps one day you'll be asked to compile *your* football annual and then you'll understand what a kick I get out of it – if you know what I mean!

When I was a boy I would spend my pocket-money on football books and hope that I'd get a good variety at Christmas, or for my birthday. When I wasn't playing I was reading about my favourites.

⚽ George was tops

Top of that list was George Best, for me the greatest player there's ever been. Many of you reading these words may wonder who George Best was. You may have heard of him but never realised just how talented he was, but he had everything a player needs: speed, skill, strength and guts. He was special.

I only saw George when he was on television, or for the once-a-year match when Manchester United came to St James's Park to play Newcastle, or to Roker Park for the game against Sunderland, and I would go along and watch him in action. That was always a great thrill.

So when I sat down to think of who would be included in my annual I decided that the book would have pictures and stories about players *I* wanted to be in its pages. These are my favourites and I hope they're yours too. Top of my list is George. I wonder who'll be top of yours when you compile your annual 20 years from now?

Enjoy the book and your football.

Bryan Robson
Captain of Manchester United and England

AUGUST

PARTIES, PROMISES, PROPHESIES

There's no better way to start a football season than with a birthday party . . . and what a swell party it was. A hundred years of the Football League gave us the chance to stage the Mercantile Credit Centenary Classic at Wembley and the fans loved it.

⚽ A swell party

With the new season just around the corner the world's top players – with a few exceptions – were on show in front of a 61,000 crowd at Wembley and a world-wide television audience.

And nobody was more thrilled than I was to captain the Football League side against a Rest of the World squad. Managed by Terry Venables, it included players like Diego Maradona, Michel Platini and our own Gary Lineker, who played for the opposition be-cause he didn't qualify as a

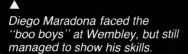

▲
Diego Maradona faced the "boo boys" at Wembley, but still managed to show his skills.

Portuguese super-star, Paulo Futre, races goalwards as Bryan gets ready to challenge. ▶

League player now he's with Barcelona.

⚽ United's day

It was quite a day for Manchester United – I managed to grab a couple of goals, Norman White-side scored another and Paul McGrath had a superb game, almost taking the Man of the Match award away from Platini.

Final score: Football League 3, Rest of the World 0, not a bad curtain raiser!

⚽ Season's kick-off

After that it was down to the nitty gritty as the 1988-89 season as everyone prepared for the big kick-off on 15 August.

The footballing fortune-tellers predicted that "Liverpool will struggle without Rush" . . . "Spurs will end the Merseyside reign" . . . "Maradona will play in England" . . . and "Manchester City will bounce straight back".

⚽ Anfield closed

The only struggling Liverpool seemed to be doing was getting Anfield ready for their first home game. Building work behind the Kop caused problems and the Scousers' opening games against Charlton and Derby had to be rearranged.

Liverpool beat Arsenal 2-1 at Highbury to get their machine rolling, Nottingham Forest won by the same scoreline at Charlton and Coventry showed that the 198_ FA Cup Final result had been no fluke when they beat Tottenham 2-1 at home.

By the end of the month Manchester United topped the First Division, but we knew that Liverpool had games in hand on everyone, and had got off to an incredible start, winning their second away game 4-1 at Coventry to show that their enforced Anfield absence was causing no real problems.

Ooops Pompey!

New boys Portsmouth found the going tough in Division One. They lost their opening game 4-2 at Watford, then went down 3-0 to Chelsea in their first home game, drew with local rivals South-ampton 2-2, were thrashed 6-0 at Highbury by a revived Arsenal side, and finally picked up their first win by beating West Ham 2-1 at Fratton Park, to the relief of Alan Ball. "We have enough quality in the side to survive in the First Division . . . don't worry about us," was his retort to criticism.

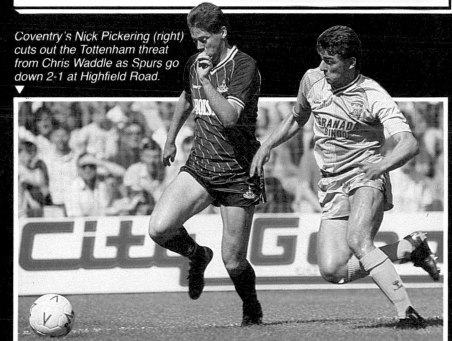

Coventry's Nick Pickering (right) cuts out the Tottenham threat from Chris Waddle as Spurs go down 2-1 at Highfield Road.

Barclays League Division One

	P	W	D	L	F	A	Pts
Manchester United	5	3	2	0	10	4	11
Queens Park Rangers	4	3	1	0	7	5	10
Tottenham Hotspur	5	3	1	1	9	4	10
Nottingham Forest	4	3	1	0	4	1	10
Chelsea	5	3	0	2	9	5	9

What, no Liverpool?

SEPTEMBER

OLÉ THE LADS!

As September started football was buzzing with a new name – Francisco Ernani Lima da Silva.

You may not recognise it straight away, and you can be forgiven for not chanting his name if you support Newcastle, but you will know who I'm talking about when I tell you that the man with the long handle is Mirandinha, the Brazilian Geordie!

⚽ **Deena's debut**

Deena, as the lads from St James's Park tagged him, made his debut for the club I supported as a boy when they played Norwich on 1 September, and he scored his first goals for Newcastle when he came to Old Trafford 11 days later and we drew 2-2.

But the sleeping giant had awakened. Liverpool played their first home game on 12 September and beat Oxford 2-0, following three days later with a 3-2 win over Charlton. The chase was on.

⚽ **European hopes**

Interest outside our domestic football focused on the European competitions and on one tie in particular. Merthyr Tydfil, very much the minnows of the Cup Winners' Cup, were drawn against Italian giants Atalanta – and beat them 2-1 in the first leg. Could the little Welsh club get to the second round?

Unfortunately not – they lost 2-0 in Italy a fortnight after their moment of glory, but they were far from disgraced.

Up in Scotland Glasgow Rangers fought back from being one down in the first leg of the European Cup to beat Dynamo

◄ *The Samba-dancing Geordie, Mirandinha, brought his Brazilian magic to Newcastle.*

Kiev 2-0 at Ibrox, thanks to goals from English exile Mark Falco and Ally McCoist. But their neighbours Celtic were knocked out of the UEFA Cup by Borussia Dortmund as Aberdeen and Dundee United scraped through.

All we could do was look on enviously from the English side of the border as the UEFA ban continued, but there was some hope of it being lifted, according to reports from certain quarters.

⚽ Trouble brewing

The Second Division pacemakers by the end of the month were Bradford City, the club so badly affected by the fire tragedy of 1985.

Things were tight in the Third Division with Wigan, Northampton, Fulham and Walsall fighting for the top spot, while in Division Four the new boys Scarborough were showing everybody that they were worthy of their League status by topping the table.

However, the black side of soccer had reared its head with outbreaks of violence, and poor Scarborough found themselves the target of the game's most unwelcome element.

RED (HOT) TAPE

At Manchester United we have a professional video set-up with a team of cameramen who record every game. Two days after we had drawn with Newcastle our video man had a phone call asking for a copy of the tape. The caller obviously wanted to study Newcastle's approach to set pieces as their goals came from a corner and a free kick, so we sent him one. The caller was Kenny Dalglish, and in Liverpool's next game they beat Newcastle 4-1 at St James's Park.

Liverpool fans please note!

Plastic topped

Queens Park Rangers, the men from plastic pitchland in London, found themselves riding high at the top of Division One. Eight wins and one draw in their first ten outings confirmed that Jim Smith's magic touch was working at Loftus Road. The only defeat Rangers suffered was at Jim's former club Oxford, but as we all know, football's a funny old game!

On top of the World. That's the feeling at Merthyr Tydfil (left) as the Welsh wonders celebrate their victory over Atalanta, in the first leg of their European clash. QPR's John Byrne (above) had the same feeling as Rangers led the First Division.

OCTOBER

▲
Ron Atkinson – in charge again at West Brom.

Big Ron & El Tel are back

It was just like old times seeing photographs of my pal Big Ron standing outside the Hawthorns. Ron Atkinson was back in charge of the club he left to manage Manchester United, and it was good to see him at West Brom in the role he filled when I played there.

◄ Hat-trick man, Gary Lineker, under pressure from Erhan of Turkey during England's 8-0 win.

⚽ Albion's saviour

Ron's task? To lift Albion away from the lower reaches of Division Two and to restore some of the charisma he generated there once before.

Ron's move to West Brom ended regular speculation that he was heading for the sunshine of Spain – his name having been linked to just about every club in the Spanish League.

⚽ October storms

Domestically October provided the second-leg games in the Little-woods Cup and some shocks.

West Ham were hammered at Upton Park by Second Division Barnsley, who won 5-2 in extra time after a two-all scoreline at the end of 180 minutes.

Southampton were toppled 3-2 on aggregate by their Division Two neighbours Bournemouth and just down the road Portsmouth bowed out 6-2 after two games with Lou Macari's Swindon Town.

Chelsea's Gordon Durie scored a hat-trick against Reading at Stamford Bridge, but the club lying one place above bottom in Division Two pulled off another surprise by scoring twice themselves and winning 5-4 over the two legs.

⚽ England in Europe

But the scoreline I enjoyed most of all in October was no surprise to anyone in the England squad: England 8 Turkey 0 in our European Championship qualifying game at Wembley.

That night we went out to show everyone that we were determined to get to the finals in West Germany, and five of us shared the goals between us with Gary Lineker getting another hat-trick. There's been plenty of talk about

Scotland's 2-0 win in Belgium, thanks to goals from Ally McCoist and Paul McStay, gave the Republic of Ireland a chance of reaching the European Championship finals. With Paul McGrath and Kevin Moran scoring the goals in a 2-0 win over Bulgaria at Lansdowne Road, the Irish turned Scotland supporters knowing that if they could beat Bulgaria in Sofia by the same scoreline then the Irish would qualify. Sound a bit confusing? Well, I'm saying nothing.

Scots boost Irish

Gary overtaking Bobby Charlton's record of 49 goals for England and I'm sure that he has every chance, especially when he gets them in threes.

John Barnes scored twice, Peter Beardsley and Neil Webb got one each and yours truly got the other as we made sure that there would be no nail-biting finish to that one!

Our Under-21 side could only draw 1-1 with the Turks in their championship game, which showed that Turkey's standard of football is improving and they may be a force to be reckoned with in the future.

⚽ Liverpool top

In Barclays League Division One Liverpool went to the top for the first time with 25 points from a possible 27. It certainly looked as if it was going to be some season for Kenny Dalglish's formidable side.

TEL GETS HIS SPURS

Barcelona ended Terry Venables' contract after only a handful of games in the 1987-88 season and with David Pleat parting company with Tottenham 'El Tel' was the man for the Spurs job. Spurs were slipping out of touch with the leaders and Venables, saying he'd start in December, promised: "I'll do my best to put this club right back at the top where it should be."

NOVEMBER

▲
Paul Stewart's goals for Manchester City had the big clubs reaching for their cheque books.

Manchester City had them reaching for the record books on 7 November as the goals began to pile up against Huddersfield Town – four-nil at half time . . . five . . . six . . . seven . . . where would it end?

City hit ten, leaving new Huddersfield manager Malcolm MacDonald stunned.

''I can't remember anything like it,'' said the player who once scored all five goals for England in a game against Cyprus at Wembley.

That's not surprising because it was the biggest winning margin in City's history, taking the place in the records of the 11-3 defeat of Lincoln City in 1895, and I'm sure Malcolm doesn't remember so far back!

⚽ A hat-trick of hat-tricks

The win boosted the hopes of City's young players, most of them coming from the club's Youth Team, drafted in by new team-manager Mel Machin.

One who didn't was Paul Stewart, one of three players to grab hat-tricks in that bumper win. He was bought from Blackpool for £200,000 but his goal-

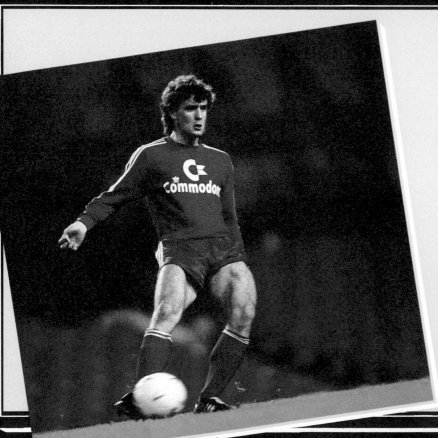

Mark my words

Mark Hughes became the target of speculation after he played for Bayern Munich in the Mercantile Credit Centenary Challenge game against Everton at Goodison Park. Sparky scored a beauty and sparked off paper talk that he'd be coming back to England before very long.

Everton were obviously impressed by the Welsh striker despite their 3-1 win but Alex Ferguson issued a hands-off warning about United's ex-player. ''I will do everything within my power to bring Mark back to Old Trafford,'' he said. It seems as if things haven't worked out for Mark since Terry Venables took him to Barcelona.

scoring was drawing in scouts from the big clubs. City's other hat-trick heroes were Tony Adcock and David White, with Neil McNab scoring a single goal. Another twist in the tale was that Huddersfield's lone goal came from a former City player, Andy May, who scored with a penalty in the 89th minute – and City still managed their tenth after that.

City stole the headlines while the top clubs in Division One had a day off. This was because of England's vital European Championship game in Belgrade where a goal-less draw would see us through.

West Germany here we come. John Barnes battles with Stojkovic of Yugoslavia as England romp home with a 4-1 win in Belgrade.

⚽ Slavs slammed

We had other ideas. Peter Beardsley took advantage of a terrible mess in the Yugoslav defence in the third minute to make it 1-0, John Barnes scored with a super free-kick, I grabbed the next with a left-foot shot, and Tony Adams made it 4-0 at half-time with his first ever international goal.

The Yugoslavs were shattered. Their supporters gave them plenty of stick and even though they pulled back a goal in the second half we were through and nobody was going to stop us.

I was thrilled to bits for the boss. Bobby Robson seems to get so much criticism and yet he has done a great job for England, taking us to the World Cup and the European Championships and he's a great man to play for.

⚽ Arsenal lead

As the end of the month approached a new name went to the top of Division One as Arsenal won at Norwich and Liverpool came to Old Trafford for the annual battle between Manchester and Merseyside. John Aldridge, the League's top scorer, put Liverpool ahead but we came back and Norman Whiteside equalised in front of 47,000 and a TV audience.

The four divisional leaders at the end of November were Arsenal, Bradford City, Sunderland and Wolves, and the bottom four Charlton, Huddersfield, York City and Newport County.

...GOALS GALORE!

DECEMBER

Elton John

Castles in the air... Sandpies in Dubai

One of the biggest talking points as the season reached its half-way stage was Elton John's announcement that he was planning to sell his shares in Watford. This must have been a difficult decision for Elton to make because we all know how much he loves his club, and it certainly sparked off a storm.

Robert Maxwell was the man ready to take over at Vicarage Road, but the Football League stepped in and decided that because of his family interests in Oxford and Derby County, they couldn't allow him to get a grip on another major club.

⚽ Maxwell maddened

This didn't surprise many people, but it angered Maxwell and he used the pages of his newspaper to tell the world of his feelings. I suppose that it could have caused problems in the future and the League had to take steps to avoid them. One example put forward was what would happen if Derby, Oxford or Watford were playing one another in a vital relegation game knowing that if they got a point they would be safe. Probably something which might never happen, but the League had to make sure that nobody could be put in this position.

⚽ Transfer time

The season reached its half way point at the end of the month with Liverpool still out in front and there

▲
Alex Ferguson's third buy of the season – central defender Steve Bruce.

Everton's Dave Watson scores in Dubai. The game ended 2-2 and Rangers won the penalty shoot-out. ▶

was some interesting activity in the transfer market.

My boss Alex Ferguson was the front runner, bringing Steve Bruce to Old Trafford from Norwich City, and what a great lad Steve turned out to be. Not only is he a good solid defender, but he has a smashing sense of humour and to top it all he's a Geordie like me. Mind you, neither of us was very chuffed when United lost at Newcastle on 26 December. It spoilt our Christmas, I can tell you!

Graeme Souness was at it again. A month after bringing Ray Wilkins back to Britain after his time in Italian and French football

he sold Mark Falco to QPR, then let another of his strikers go to Norwich as the Canaries spent some of the money they'd got from United on Robert Fleck.

Rangers 'Champions'

Rangers also took the unofficial title of British champions when they beat Everton in a unique match. It wasn't played at Ibrox or Goodison, plans to stage the game at Maine Road had to be

shelved and it was eventually held in Dubai! I suppose a bit of sunshine in December was the aim although the game itself had to be settled on penalties.

While Everton were heading home from the Middle East Nottingham Forest picked up their first trophy of the season when they won the Football League Soccer Six tournament in Manchester. They beat us in the final in a shoot-out after a rip-roaring three nights of non-stop football.

Division Two							
	P	W	D	L	F	A	Pts
Middlesbrough	22	13	5	4	33	14	44
Bradford City	22	13	4	5	36	25	43
Aston Villa	22	11	7	4	33	20	40
Division Three							
	P	W	D	L	F	A	Pts
Sunderland	20	11	6	3	40	19	39
Notts County	20	10	7	3	37	23	37
Walsall	20	10	7	3	30	18	37

North-east going strong

The North-East's soccer future was looking brighter at the half-way stage in the season. Middlesbrough hammered out their intention by leading the Second Division and Sunderland topped the Third.

I've always been a believer that there should be a soccer stronghold in that area just as there was a few years ago, and it's great to see those two clubs doing so well.

JANUARY

▲
Brian Clough – his comments made the headlines.

Charlie Nicholas went back to Scotland to try to pick up his career. After Celtic, his Arsenal days were difficult. ▶

Bonnie Prince Charlie rides north

Charlie Nicholas – the darling of some Arsenal supporters – delayed his New Year celebrations by a few days as he moved back to Scotland to join Aberdeen in a £400,000 transfer which caught the headlines on both sides of the border.

Arsenal boss George Graham took a cheque for £400,000 from Aberdeen and some unwarranted stick from other managers, including Brian Clough, who got himself into hot water by saying that George was barmy!

Cloughie isn't one for mincing words, but he faced a rap from the football authorities for the remark.

Barmy or not, Charlie showed that he thought the transfer was a good idea in a great debut. It ended goal-less but Charlie must think touching wood is lucky because he hit the Hibernian crossbar twice at Easter Road.

▲
Dave Bassett – could he save the Blades?

◄ Cup tussle of the month. Sheffield Wednesday's Lawrie Madden beats Everton's Wayne Clarke in this challenge, but the Merseysiders had the last laugh.

⚽ Cup shockers

The top clubs forgot the League for a moment to turn their attention to the FA Cup, and little Stoke almost pulled off a shocker when they drew 0-0 with Liverpool in round three, but lost the replay. Everton and Sheffield Wednesday got themselves involved in a marathon and we beat Ipswich at Portman Road.

Everton got to round five the hardest way. They had three games with Wednesday before sorting things out, and then they pulled off a remarkable victory at Hillsbrough, thanks to a Graeme Sharp hat-trick and goals from Adrian Heath and Ian Snodin.

But the real shocker was at Vale Park in the fifth round when Port Vale beat mighty Tottenham 2-1 – not a day to remember for Spurs, but that's what the FA Cup's all about. It isn't so good when you're on the losing end, but those Port Vale lads must have enjoyed themselves that night!

⚽ Bassett goes north

Dave Bassett, the man who took Wimbledon from obscurity to the First Division, was one of the first managers to change his job in 1988. Dave packed it in at Vicarage Road after all the traumas of the sell-out, and ten days later was back in work, this time at Bramall Lane, in charge of struggling Sheffield United. Dave is one of those managers who seems to be able to inspire players, so it will be interesting to see what he can do with the Blades.

One of the first things that Watford did after Dave's exit was to beat cup holders Coventry at Highfield Road . . . and Elton decided not to sell after all.

FEBRUARY

MUNICH MEMORIES, MAULINGS AND MISSES

Saturday, 6 February marked the 30th anniversary of the Munich air disaster. A lot of young people don't know what happened on that day but if I tell you that eight Manchester United players were killed, two were so badly injured they never played again, and eight top sports writers also died together with club officials, you can see why the event was so momentous.

We commemorated it with a minute's silence before the game with Coventry, and the supporters of both clubs showed tremendous respect. You could have heard a pin drop at Old Trafford, and it illustrated to me that there are still a lot of decent people in football.

Incidentally, we won 1-0 and Liam O'Brien's goal was scored at four minutes past three – the exact time of the crash.

 **Gazza job**

The picture of the month, if not the season, has got to be the one which brought a smile to everyone's face – with the exception of Paul Gascoigne. His tussle with Vinnie Jones in the League clash with Wimbledon had everyone wondering what the Don's hard man will get up to next, and with the clubs thrown together in the FA Cup there wasn't long to wait, but Newcastle were knocked out in front of their own supporters.

I was choked to miss our cup tie with Arsenal. I'd strained a thigh muscle during a bit of shooting practice with Peter Shilton in Tel Aviv before the mid-week friendly with Israel, and on the morning of the cup tie I did it again during a fitness check. So I had to watch as Arsenal led 2-0 at half time and United fought back with a goal from Brian McClair before the vital penalty in the last minutes.

Brian missed as he was trying to blast for the top corner, but he shouldered the responsibility and stood up to face his critics.

February's top tie was the

Merseyside clash at Goodison, and Liverpool made amends for their defeat in the Littlewoods Cup by winning 1-0, thanks to a Ray Houghton goal.

⚽ Everton out again

It was a bad week for Everton as Arsenal booked themselves a place at Wembley thanks to a second-leg win in the Littlewoods Cup semi-final to give them a 4-1 aggregate. The Gunners' goals came from Michael Thomas, David Rocastle and Alan Smith, but Martin Hayes missed a penalty in exactly the same way Brian McClair missed his, so now he knows what it feels like!

Sounds familiar, doesn't it?

Tommy Docherty lost his 18th job in football on 4 February when he was sacked as manager of non-League Altrincham. The Doc, whose career had taken him to Chelsea, Rotherham, QPR (twice), Aston Villa, Hull City, Manchester United, Derby County, Preston, Wolves, Oporto, Melbourne, Sydney Olympic and the Scotland manager's job said: "I used to joke that I'd had more clubs than Jack Nicklaus, but golfers can only carry fourteen!"

Doc added that he's had enough – and who can blame him?

▲ David Rocastle – helped Arsenal get to Wembley.

◀ Anfield ace, John Barnes, helps out Neil Webb as England attack in Tel Aviv. Israel's challengers are former Liverpool star Avi Cohen (left) and Avraham Cohen.

◀ *Barcelona bound? Howard Kendall stayed in Bilbao.*

The brush-off

Another minor detail which is also important, gave United some unwanted – and incorrect – publicity early in the month.

It was bad enough losing 1-0 to Norwich and feeling the strength of Alex Ferguson's anger, but the next morning we were stunned to read that the Boss had made us sweep out the dressing room as a punishment.

True, we had cleaned up after the game, which is one of the minor details Alex Ferguson insists on, but it was our kit man Norman Davies who swept up, and not the players.

Apparently what happened is that the Norwich apprentices who normally clean the dressing rooms went to do their job, saw ours was clean and said, "Fergie must've made them sweep it out." A press man overheard, and the rest you know.

Liverpool lose

What was fact during March was that Forest, Luton and Wimbledon all got through to the semi-finals of the FA Cup, as Liverpool went to Maine Road to face the youngsters of Manchester City.

Some felt that City might just pull it off. Liverpool were a game away from equalling Leeds United's record of 29 unbeaten League games from the start of a season, City were struggling but might rise to the occasion.

That was wishful thinking, as Liverpool ran riot, winning 4-0 on a rainy afternoon, with goals from Ray Houghton, Peter Beardsley, John Barnes and Craig Johnston.

Three days later Liverpool equalled the record with a 1-1 draw at Derby, but a week after the cup win the run ended, and at Goodison Park of all places. Liverpool were beaten by a Wayne Clarke goal, and his brother Alan was a member of the Leeds record breakers of the seventies.

March madness...

We've all heard of the mad March hare so I suppose I can forgive a bit of craziness creeping in this month. At least, that's a reasonable excuse for some of the daft headlines which filled the sports pages during March, with two of them way off target.

"Kendall accepts Barcelona job," said one; "United stars sweep out dressing room" was another.

Result: Fact 2 Headlines 0!

...makes news

The former Everton boss signed another 12-month contract with Bilbao, the side he's managed since emigrating, but he *was* tempted by a massive cash offer from big-spending Barcelona.

"I came here to do a job for Bilbao," he said, "and I want to do that job."

Another thing Howard said which caught my eye was that two years earlier he had been for an interview with Barcelona, and they still hadn't paid his train fare from Liverpool to London. A minor detail, perhaps, but if you forget little things, what about important issues?

MARCH

Dread-locky

Holland gave us a taste of what to expect in the European Championships when Ruud Gullit, the former European Footballer of the Year with the dreadlock hair-style, paved the way for a 2-2 draw.

Gullit laid on a super second goal for John Bosman after earlier forcing Tony Adams to turn the ball into his own net.

Gary Lineker got his 24th England goal in 24 starts, and Adams made amends for his enforced error with the equaliser.

Did he fall or was he pushed? Liverpool's Craig Johnston sprawls as Paul Lake recovers from the challenge. Result: a penalty against Manchester City.

Graeme Sharp celebrates as Wayne Clarke's goal ends Liverpool's record run.

APRIL

No Fools this April

Nothing in football is as simple as it seems. Just ask Liverpool. On 1 April they were being hotly tipped to take the League Championship before Easter and three days later had collected just one point out of a possible six, their worst spell of the season!

Liverpool were no April Fools, but they fell to Brian Clough's Nottingham Forest in the craziest way.

Alan Hansen scored first for Forest, Bruce Grobbelaar saved a Nigel Clough penalty, and the Anfield spot king John Aldridge put Liverpool back in the game after Neil Webb had made it 2-0 just on the hour.

It could be that Liverpool's thoughts were on a game that was a week away, but that second defeat of the season meant that they couldn't secure the title when they met us at Anfield on Easter Monday.

What a game that was. I scored in the second minute, then Liverpool stormed into a 3-1 lead just after half-time but we fought back to level 3-3 — and that was after having Colin Gibson sent off!

 Gazza goes too

Colin wasn't alone. Paul Gascoigne also got his marching orders as Newcastle lost at Derby the same afternoon. That was Gazza's second sending-off of the season, and he got into more hot water for kicking the trainer's bucket over as he left the field.

I suppose it's frustration that leads to things like that, and I know that Paul would have been more angry with himself for being sent off than he was at actually getting the red card.

He made the headlines again a day later by refusing to sign a new contract at Newcastle, and that started the guessing game about where he would finish up. Anfield? Tottenham? Old Trafford?

Another player who made it clear that he wanted a move was Norman Whiteside, and he was put on the transfer list by United after saying that he felt stale. It's a pity that Norman felt that way because he has always been a great lad to have around, but he wants to try his luck abroad and I suppose he knows best.

 More shocks

There was another shock for the Old Trafford fans a few days later when Paul McGrath also said that he wanted to leave, and as club policy is not to stand in the way of anyone whose heart is not 100 per cent with United, he too was listed.

All the speculation was forgotten by the end of that week when, shock of shocks, Wimbledon got through to the FA Cup Final. They did it in style, beating Luton 2-1 after fighting back from behind.

▲ John Barnes fulfils my dream – he has his hands on the League Championship trophy

◄ The flaw in Gazza's game – he's about to get his marching orders for the second time in the 1987-88 season

Everyone felt that they would stand no chance at Wembley against Liverpool who had beaten Forest in their semi-final at Hillsbrough, with Aldo scoring from the spot yet again!

While all this had been going on, Wolves were making promotion look a cert in the Fourth Division, Sunderland were going great guns in the Third and the battle at the top of the Second reached boiling point with Millwall creeping up on everyone as Blackburn, Aston Villa and Bradford City began to slip up.

Brian McClair reached a career milestone when he scored his 20th League goal of the season against Luton, the first Manchester United player to hit this mark since George Best in 1968.

⚽ Liverpool double favourites

But Liverpool's championship intentions were clear. They slammed Forest 5-0 at Anfield as the Nottingham chairman Maurice Roworth said: "No team in Europe could have competed with them on this

Top *Action from the Mercantile Credit Football League Centenary Festival at Wembley as Wolves take on Everton*

Above *The parade of clubs at Wembley was a colourful affair*

form". Two more points and the title would be theirs.

It came against Tottenham on 23 April, a week after the Centenary Festival at Wembley saw them losing to Newcastle in the first round, and with the Cup Final coming up Liverpool were red hot favourites for the double.

Before the month ended we had a trip abroad with England, to play Hungary in Budapest and although it was a goal-less draw we were satisfied with our performance which was good preparation for the European Championships. Gary Pallister made his debut and played well at centre-back.

That game was four days after the first domestic cup final of the season when Luton pipped Arsenal in the Littlewoods Cup and what a thriller that was, illustrating to the Gunners that as I said earlier, nothing is as simple as it seems!

The unacceptable face of football – mounted police guard Chelsea supporters following their relegation playoff defeat against Middlesbrough.

MAY *THUGS* ...spoil celebrations

May is traditionally the month when football's winners and losers are sorted out, but in May 1988 the game itself looked like being a loser, thanks to the behaviour of so-called soccer fans.

We had the worry that hooligans were going to disrupt the European Championships, violence at the England-Scotland game at Wembley, then disgusting scenes when Chelsea were relegated in the play-offs.

There were brighter things to remember though, with Millwall stepping into the First Divison for the first time in their history as Division Two champions, joined by Aston Villa, then wonder club Middlesbrough, the conquerors of Chelsea.

 Not the first

Boro became the first club to get into the top section through the modern-day play offs, but did you know that in 1894 that is how Liverpool first got into Division One? They had what were called Test Matches in the early days of the game and sorted out the ups and downs in play-off games. Liverpool went up and Newton Heath went down . . . and Newton Heath later altered their name to Manchester United!

Things have changed a lot since then, but Liverpool pipped United again in 1988.

Middlesbrough's victories over Bradford City and then Chelsea ended the fairytale revival of the club which looked like going bust a few years ago — what a brilliant job Bruce Rioch has done at Ayrsome Park! I'm looking forward to the chance of playing against another club from the north-east, where the game is going through a revival.

Sunderland up too

Sunderland won promotion as Third Division champions, which can only be good news for the lads from Roker Park, and if they can emulate Boro and get up to Division One in 1989 that will be smashing.

I've dealt with the FA Cup final elsewhere but with May being the month for celebration it's also the time of the year when clubs have got to pick themselves up after a disappointment.

Liverpool will do that without any problems, but I think that Lincoln City are the best example of what football spirit is all about.

They were the first club to be relegated from the League in 1987 when the new promotion and relegation spot from the Vauxhall Conference was introduced, and what did Lincoln do? They bounced straight back, pulling in the biggest crowds the Conference has seen, and now they can only go upwards.

Help them back

Others who went down with Chelsea were Oxford, Portsmouth and Watford, but with good well-

▲ *Wolves snap back – two years after being on the brink of extinction Graham Turner and his players celebrate Wolves' Sherpa Van Trophy success. Wolves also won the Fourth Division title.*

behaved support they too can bounce back and that should be the aim of every club and every supporter. If you have any pride in your game you should make your club proud of you.

The Second Division said goodbye to Millwall, Aston Villa and Middlesbrough who went up, but also to Sheffield Wednesday who were relegated along with Huddersfield and Reading.

Brighton were promoted to the Second, and Cardiff and Bolton joined Wolves as they stepped

out of the Fourth Division. While York, Doncaster and Grimsby slid down to the bottom section it was Newport County who found themselves out of the League and with perhaps the toughest task for the new season . . . survival.

Jim Leighton

The big signing of the month was a new team-mate for me, Jim Leighton the Aberdeen goalkeeper, who joined United for £750,000, a club record for a keeper. Jim showed me that the fee was justified when he faced us in the England-Scotland game – he was brilliant. I'm looking forward to more performances like that from him . . . but when we're on the same side!

PAUL GASGOIGNE

Gazza's after my England place... but he'll have to wait!

There isn't any doubt that Newcastle's Paul Gascoigne is going to have a tremendous future in the game.

Gazza plays for my boyhood favourites Newcastle United and I've got every confidence that he's the one who's going to challenge me for my England place in the future. Mind you I've no intention of letting that go for a while, but Paul is destined for plenty of honours.

I think Paul's got everything you need to be a top class player. He has great ability, although one of his weaknesses may be that he is just a little temperamental at present. Like a lot of managers I like to see players with a bit of devilment in them, Paul's got that, and coupled with his skills it makes him an outstanding prospect.

 Still learning

Paul still has a lot to learn, but his knowledge of the game will increase as he gets older and, having already established himself in the First Division, all he has to do now is to mature, develop those skills and curb the spirit so that he continues to play with fire yet stays out of trouble.

Getting sent off doesn't help a player and Paul's been in hot water more than once; this sort of thing can give you a reputation, justified or not, that's hard to live with. I'm not saying that referees judge players by their records, but they're only human and must be influenced by what they've read in the papers or seen on TV.

Gazza's a bit similar to Norman Whiteside in a way. I don't think that he's as hard as Norman, but he has the same winner's attitude which can lead to over aggressiveness. If he can just curb that the way Norman has done, he'll be a better player for it.

Paul Gascoigne leaves Liverpool's Great Dane Jan Molby bemused and beaten on the ground as he sets off towards goal

> "Paul Gascoigne has a bright future in front of him and there's no reason why he shouldn't make it to the top. He has skill, strength and above all a will to win. These are essentials in a player. You need heart to succeed in football and Gazza has plenty of that."

He likes a joke

Paul's a great lad. I've met him a couple of times when he's been with the England Under 21 squad and he struck me as being a smashing sort of bloke. He's jolly and enjoys a joke and I only hope that too much media attention doesn't spoil him.

I tend to think that the newspapers build players up so that they can simply knock them down again and I hope that they don't do that to Paul, because I don't know how he'd handle it.

Paul's been criticised because he gets overweight from time to time. The only advice I would offer him is that while he's young there's nothing wrong with having a chocolate bar and the occasional bottle of Newcastle's famous brown ale, provided he trains hard. (While you're young you can more or less eat anything and burn off the extra weight with exercise.) But as Paul gets older he'll have to be more careful.

Born: Gateshead
Club: Newcastle United
Debut: 1985
Honours: FA Youth Cup winner's medal 1985
International honours: England Under 21
Position: Midfield

FIVE FOR THE FUTURE

NIGEL CLOUGH

Nigel's a chip off the Clough block

If I had been asked to name the player I felt had improved the most over the past year I would have had only one choice, Nigel Clough of Nottingham Forest.

What a smashing player he's become in a short time and I reckon that we are going to hear a lot of him in the years to come.

It is surely only a matter of time before Nigel emulates his dad and wins full international honours
▼

I suppose that one of the things which has helped him has been an all-round improvement in the Forest side, as manager Brian Clough has once again created a squad that is good enough to challenge for the championship.

Nigel strikes me as being one of those players who needs good players around him. He has such great vision that he is one step ahead of the ordinary player. When I bracket him with Norman Whiteside and Kenny Dalglish I might raise a few eyebrows, but only from people who don't know very much about top-level football.

When Norman played up front for Manchester United and Northern Ireland his skill with his first touch of the ball, and his reading of the game, was the closest thing that I have seen to Kenny Dalglish, who for me is the best creator and anticipator there has been in the game for many a day.

Nigel fits into this category. He may not have the pace of some front-line players, but his quick thinking and his ability to read situations ahead of the opposition makes up for that.

Kenny and Norman are the same. They can control the ball instantly and knock off a pass to a better placed colleague with one deft touch; and that is why I say that Nigel has shown how good he is because those around him have improved.

It is no use creating opportunities if there is no-one quick enough to make the best of them.

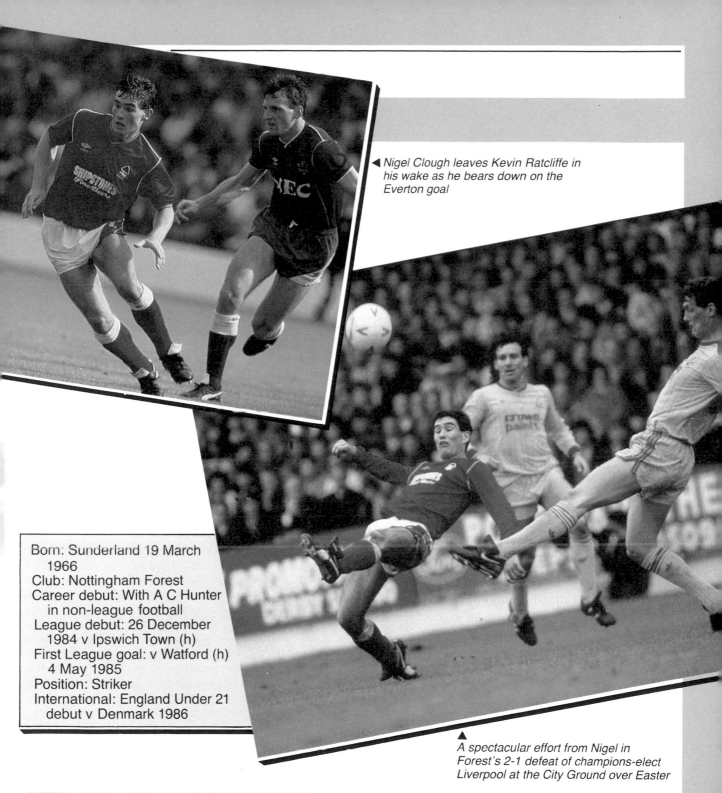

◀ Nigel Clough leaves Kevin Ratcliffe in his wake as he bears down on the Everton goal

Born: Sunderland 19 March
   1966
Club: Nottingham Forest
Career debut: With A C Hunter
   in non-league football
League debut: 26 December
   1984 v Ipswich Town (h)
First League goal: v Watford (h)
   4 May 1985
Position: Striker
International: England Under 21
   debut v Denmark 1986

▲
A spectacular effort from Nigel in Forest's 2-1 defeat of champions-elect Liverpool at the City Ground over Easter

⚽ Playing for dad

Nigel has also had to overcome the difficulty of playing for his dad. I know what footballers can be like and being the boss's son must sometimes have made life hard for Nigel in the dressing room. But he's coped brilliantly with the situation and I'm sure that his team-mates accept him for the player he is and don't even remember that his dad is their boss.

I think that it might even have worked against Nigel having dad in charge because he will most likely have had to train harder, run longer and play better than the others to avoid anyone thinking that he was being favoured!

So, far from being spoiled by dad, Nigel has turned out to be a credit to his family and his club and I am sure that he will reach the top as a player very soon and stay there for a long time.

GARY PALLISTER

Middlesbrough's Gary Pallister has got one natural gift which will make him an outstanding central defender in the future. The big man has all the usual assets – height, strength, a cool head, and the ability to read defensive situations, but on top of all that he is fast.

Gary Pallister became the first Second Division player selected by Bobby Robson for England's full international team. He took his chance well.

Speed in a big defender is such a help to a side and to the development of a player. The two fastest centre-backs that I have come across in recent years have been Kevin Ratcliffe of Everton and my own team-mate at Old Trafford for many seasons, Paul McGrath.

Gary is another who can turn up the speed when required and there are so many times during a game when this will prove a match winner – or even a point saver.

⚽ Speedy defence

How many times have you seen the big men outpaced by a nippy forward in a chase for the ball? How many strikers use their speed as a weapon against the back four, hoping to push the ball into space and then race after it? Try that with Gary Pallister and you'll probably lose!

I've met Gary quite a lot because of his introduction to the England squad at the start of 1988 and he strikes me as being a sensible lad who knows where he is going.

⚽ Proof needed

Gary has still to prove himself in the First Division, but he shouldn't find that too hard, and he had a very impressive debut for England in Budapest when we met Hungary in a friendly in April 1988.

I can see Gary being around at international level for a long time even though he got his chance to get

Boro's big hope Pallister is England's too!

1 *For a big man Pallister is more than comfortable with the ball at his feet. He also possesses a powerful shot*

2 *Having dispossessed a Hungarian attacker Gary is looking to set up an England attack in Budapest*

Born: Ramsgate 30 June 1965
Club: Middlesbrough
Career debut: With Billingham Town in non-league football.
League debut: 17 August 1985 v Wimbledon (a).
Became regular member of first team later same season
Position: Central defender
International debut: Full England v Hungary (a) 1988

3 *The perfect end to a successful season. Gary, along with Colin Cooper and Gary Hamilton, celebrate Boro's 2-1 aggregate win over Chelsea to secure promotion to the First Division.*

into the full England side only because of the unfortunate injury Terry Butcher had last season. Some people were calling him the new Butcher, but their games are very different.

⚽ Ball player

Gary doesn't have the aggression of Terry, but he is a good ball player. His skill on the ground is remarkable for a big man. His style of play reminds me of Liverpool's Phil Thompson in that he likes to create moves from the back and keep the ball on the ground rather than just belting it up-field in the old-fashioned centre-half style. Gary is probably faster than Phil was, but if he can achieve half the success the Liverpool man had then he won't have a bad career. We will soon see how well he can read the game at top level, and that is where his speed will pay off.

DAVID ROCASTLE

No rocky road for Rocastle, only a bright path to the top

David Rocastle's speed and skill will surely carry him to great heights in the future.

The Arsenal speed-merchant is one of the brightest long-term prospects in the game today and as far as I'm concerned he's an outstanding player.

◄ David Rocastle has the Canaries' defence in a flap as he beats off two Norwich challenges

Hard worker

He's a good hard-working lad who has come on in leaps and bounds since he got into the Arsenal side, and he is a very difficult player to face. He is always ready to get involved, and gets through a tremendous amount of work during 90 minutes.

When you play wide like David you have to be prepared to do a lot of running and he has a good engine which keeps him on the move. He has a lot of ability, and this coupled with his speed has turned him into a top-class First Division player.

If I have to pick out a weakness which perhaps David can work on in the future, I'd say that what we refer to in the game as the 'final ball' needs to be looked at. That's the ball we play in the last third of the field, the final pass of a move which can create a goal for a colleague.

David has the skill to get into situations where a goal seems certain, then he will fall down on the final ball, but that is something he has time to develop, and when he has he will be the complete wide player.

Born: Lewisham, London
Club: Arsenal
Debut: 1985-86 season
League (Littlewoods) Cup:
    Winners' medal 1987;
    Runners'-up medal 1988
International: England
    Under-21

Many gifts

He gets into the penalty area a lot and scores good goals. He's a natural athlete and obviously looks after himself, which is another important factor in any young player's development.

Usually when a player reaches 24 or 25 he achieves the standard that marks his peak. He may get better, but this is only through experience, but provided that he trains hard and learns as he goes along he will be around for a long time.

Future star

David and I haven't met much socially, although we have played against each other a few times, and my assessment of him is based purely on what I have seen either during those Arsenal-Manchester United clashes, or when he has appeared in games I've watched on TV or from the grandstand. However, you can take it from me that the name of David Rocastle is going to be as well known in footballing circles of the future as some of the stars of the past who have worn the red and white of the Gunners.

▲
David collects his first European Player of the Year award, even if it is the Gunners' Scandinavia Supporters Club Player of the Year

FIVE FOR THE FUTURE

PAUL LAKE

Versatile Lake – time will tell whether he'll bridge the gap

Only time will tell whether Paul Lake lives up to expectations or not, but I think that the Manchester City youngster is going to make it to the top.

Paul's been on the scene for two years now and has been growing in experience with every game. He's had problems with injuries, but provided that he can put these behind him I'm sure that he'll make it – and I suppose I can speak from experience when I say that!

I've seen Paul in action a few times when I've been able to go along to City's matches and he seems to have a lot of talent. He isn't outstanding at one particular aspect of the game, but he's very good at all of them. He has good control, strength and skill, and can obviously read play, which is so essential.

 ### He's versatile

That is what has made him such a versatile player – he can play virtually anywhere. He's been in the defence and in midfield and I'm sure that he can play up front just as well, which means he's really valuable to his club.

Like most of his colleagues at Maine Road, Paul's only a youngster, and should improve as the years go by. City have got youthful enthusiasm on their side and they play off this, rather than from experience, which is the backbone to sides like Liverpool.

Enthusiasm is a great thing, but sometimes it can go wrong for young players, and that is where experience comes in handy. By this I mean that you have got to learn how to handle certain situations during a game and not fall into traps put there by crafty opponents.

Born: Denton, Manchester
Club: Manchester City
FA Youth Cup: Winners' Medal
   1986; Runners'-up medal
   1987
Youth team: Captain 1986-87
League debut: v Wimbledon
   1987 (Division One)
First League goal: v Luton,
   February 1987

⚽ Learning fast

However, there's no better way to learn than out there on the field and that's the way Paul's game is developing.

The only question mark I would put against him is whether or not he will be able to perform as capably at top level. There is a big difference between a season in the First Division and a season in the Second, and with City still fighting for promotion Paul and his pals have got to wait before they can show us what they are made of.

One of Paul's biggest upsets must have been finding himself ruled out of England's Under-21 games in the European Championship last season. Every time Paul was selected he seemed to get injured. I know that it's a hard thing to take having to stay at home when you could be away with the international squad.

But his turn will come and then he'll be able to enjoy mixing with players from other clubs and other levels of the game. I'm sure that Paul Lake is going to be around for a long time.

▲
The worst sight in football as Paul is put on a stretcher. Paul has had wretched luck with injuries already

◄ *Paul Lake gets it in the neck as he wins a challenge at Simod Cup winners Reading*

LUTON HIT THE

If ever there was a perfect advert for what top-level football is all about, the 1988 Littlewoods Cup Final was just that. It was the classic cup final, a thriller from start to finish with all the drama, excitement, joy and despair you associate with Wembley and the big occasion.

Mal Donaghy shows off the Littlewoods Cup after Luton's classic win in the shoot-out with Arsenal

It was open attacking football by both sides, and there was bags of action in each goalmouth. I loved every minute of it, and didn't want the final whistle to go, and that puts it high on my list of games to remember.

I've got to give Luton the credit they deserve, because they must have felt that they were out of it when they were trailing to Arsenal, especially when the Gunners were awarded a vital penalty.

Brian Stein know what it's like to feel "over the moon" and "sick as a parrot" in the same game.

He would have been delighted to score the opening goal and when the Luton lads went into the dressing room at half-time they would have been fairly confident that they could take the cup . . . but Arsenal had other ideas.

George Graham must have told his players to keep going and the game would turn their way, and

for half an hour they dominated. Then nine minutes from time came the penalty.

I've no need to tell you that football has always been a funny old game, even before Jimmy Greaves pinched the words as his trademark.

⚽ A lesson for Nigel

As Nigel Winterburn stepped up to take the kick, my mind went back to the day we met Arsenal in the FA Cup at Highbury and an incident not many people were aware of. Brian McClair missed his spot kick, which was bad enough, but Nigel had a bit of a go at Brian and that was out of order. He had no reason to say anything, but what he did say made me furious.

So when Luton's reserve keeper Andy Dibble dived to his left and pulled off that match-winning save I felt that justice had been done. Nigel now

JACKPOT

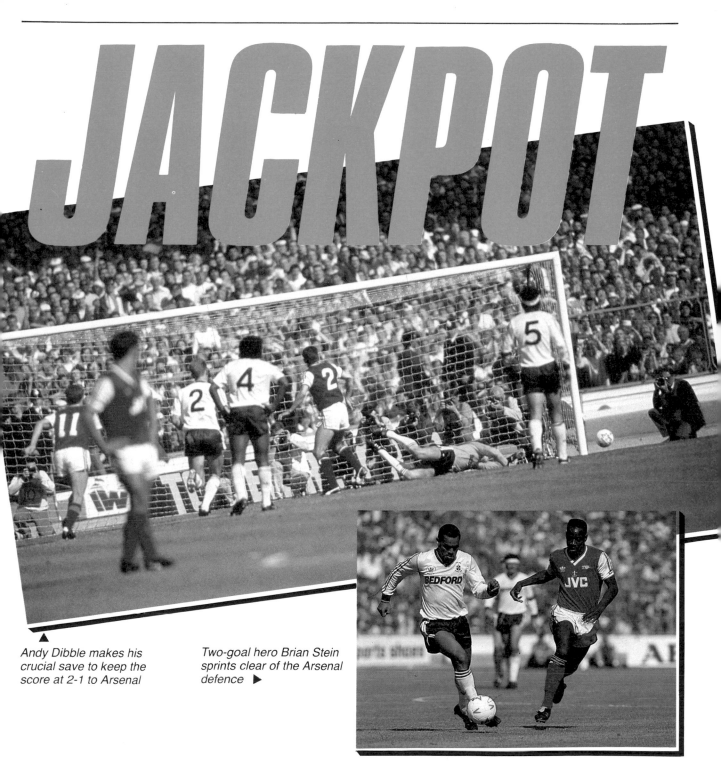

▲
Andy Dibble makes his crucial save to keep the score at 2-1 to Arsenal

Two-goal hero Brian Stein sprints clear of the Arsenal defence ▶

knows what it is like to miss a penalty on a big occasion and he will also know that he wouldn't have liked one of the Luton players to have a far from friendly word in his ear as the game re-started! It was unfortunate for him that he had to learn his lesson in front of 94,000 people at Wembley, and millions more watching the game on television.

That save was the turning point. Luton stormed back with another Brian Stein goal and one from

Danny Wilson and the cup went to Kenilworth Road.

There has always got to be a loser in a cup final and that was one of those games when both sides must have felt they were going to win and then going to lose. When it all ended the real winner was the game of football itself.

If every Wembley final was going to be like that, they would be queuing from January for the tickets! Thanks, lads, you did the game proud.

Romance 1 Football 0

but no real thriller

I know that millions of television viewers and tens of thousands of football romantics loved every minute of the 1988 FA Cup Final, but I felt it was a poor game. In saying that I don't want to take anything away from Wimbledon, who shocked everyone by beating "invincible" Liverpool, but as a game of football it was a fairly drab affair.

A lot of people were saying immediately after the final that Wimbledon deserved their win, but I'm afraid I can't agree.

I'm not knocking Dave Beasant and his pals, who did what they set out to do, but on the day I felt that neither side deserved to win

FA CUP

the Cup, and if ever there was a game which should have gone to a replay, this was it.

No clear winner

Both sides created just as many chances as the other, both had refereeing decisions going against them, and when I look back on what is supposed to be the showpiece of English football, the end of season carnival, it was a far from thrilling afternoon.

I didn't think that either side did enough to win the Cup and I'm sure the Liverpool lads will agree with me when I say that they never played anywhere near their full potential, but then neither did Wimbledon.

They were classed as underdogs, but it's a long time since they were that. They may have risen from obscurity, but they are a First Division club now, so they have earned the right to demand respect.

Worthy finalists

This was no clash between First and Fourth Division, despite the contrast in backgrounds. True, it was a battle between the millionaire club and one which struggles to keep its financial head above the water, but both teams are equal in playing football.

Wimbledon have done enough to be recognised as worthy finalists, so we can be just as critical of them as we might be had it been any other First Division club.

It was one for the romantics, but let's give Wimbledon some credit. They didn't get a free ticket to Wembley but worked their way there just like Liverpool.

Psyched? Rubbish!

There was a lot of nonsense written about the way Wimbledon "psyched" Liverpool out of their rhythm, how they scared the pants off them in the Wembley tunnel with their famous war-cry,

but I don't believe a word of that. They try it all the time — they did it with us a few days before the final, shouting their slogan about "putting it in the mixer" before we beat them at Old Trafford. But from my point of view it doesn't have any effect at all, and I can't see it putting Liverpool, with all their experience, off their stride.

Ever since I became a professional footballer I've faced opponents who shout at you, threaten you and talk to you during a game, but they're just wasting their time as far as I'm concerned and as for upsetting Liverpool — you must be joking!

So, call me a killjoy if you want to, but give me a final full of exciting action, fast-flowing football in future and you can keep your romance!

What a thrill it must have been for Dave Beasant when he became not only the first goalkeeper to save an FA Cup Final penalty at Wembley, but the first number one to go up and collect the Cup. For me Dave is one of the top six keepers in the country and he has a remarkable record with Wimbledon — the final was his 351st consecutive game. He is a model for any tall lad to follow. He is agile, uses his height to great effect and reads the game so well, and as for that penalty save . . . !

◀ *Matchwinner Lawrie Sanchez soars above Ray Houghton at Wembley*

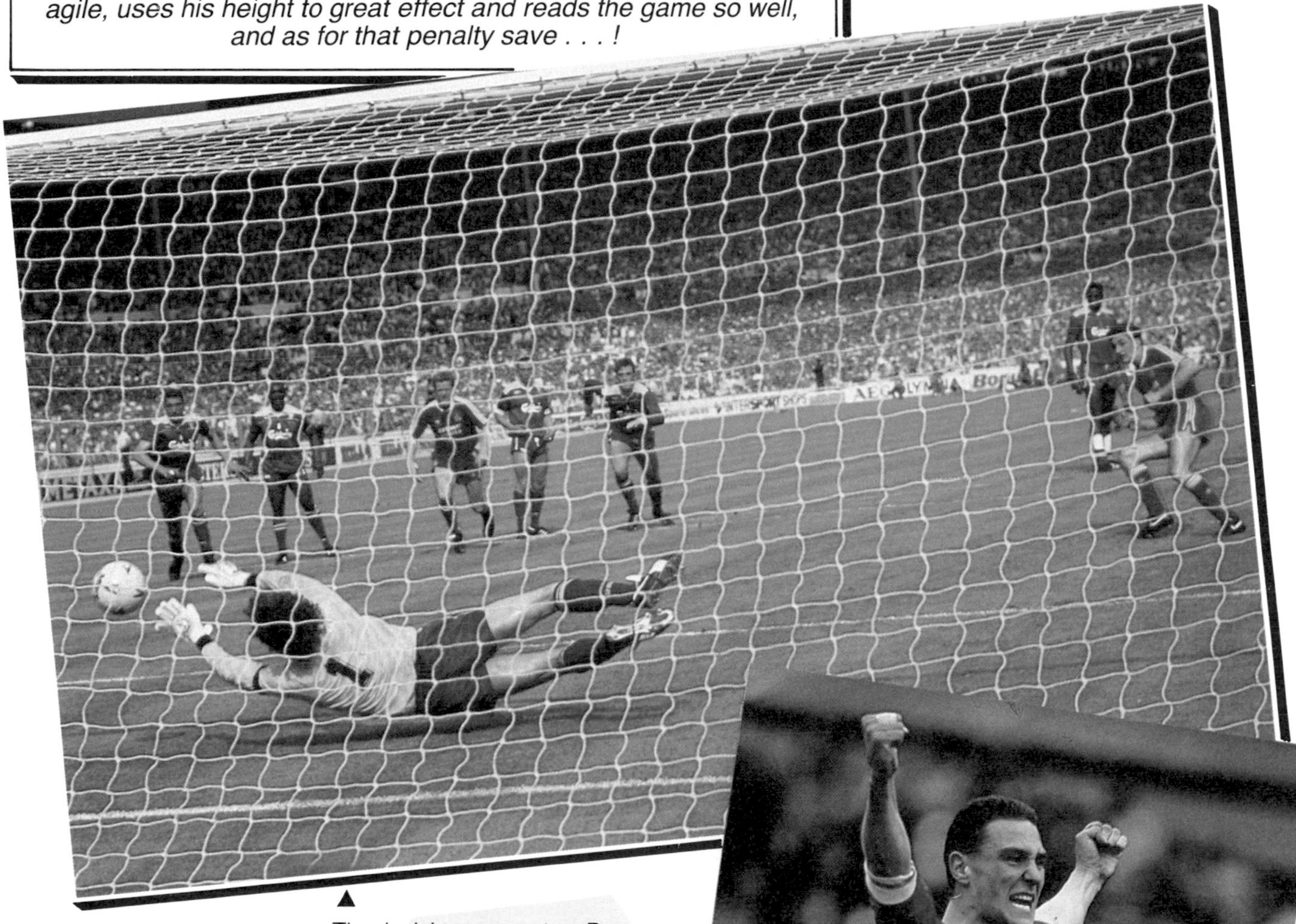

▲ *The decisive moment as Dave Beasant dives to turn John Aldridge's penalty away. The pressure on penalty takers has grown over the years – Brian McClair's miss at Highbury may have cost us a place on the hallowed turf this season*

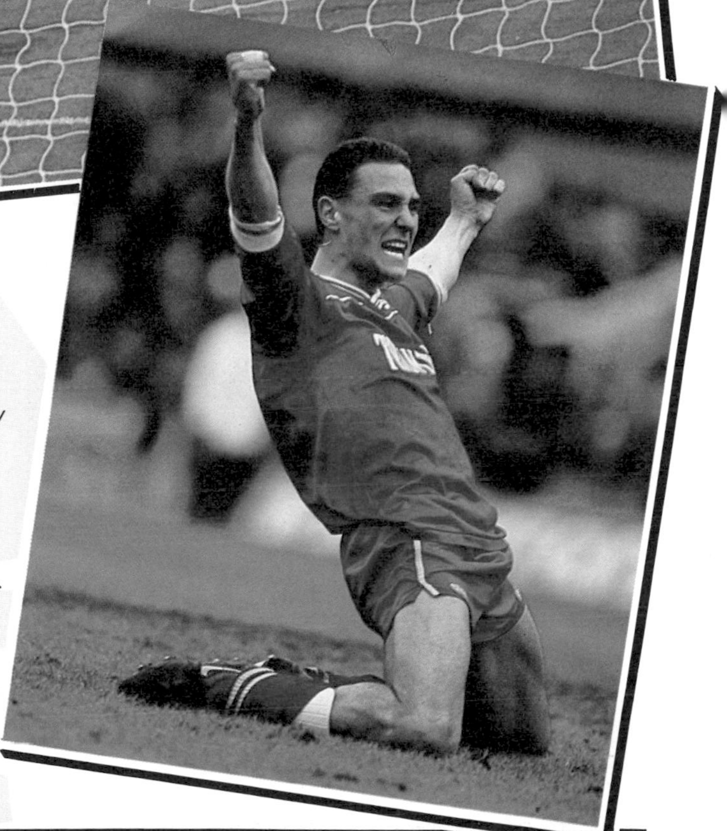

Vinny Jones celebrates the defeat of Luton which booked the Dons' place at Wembley ▶

PRIZE GUYS

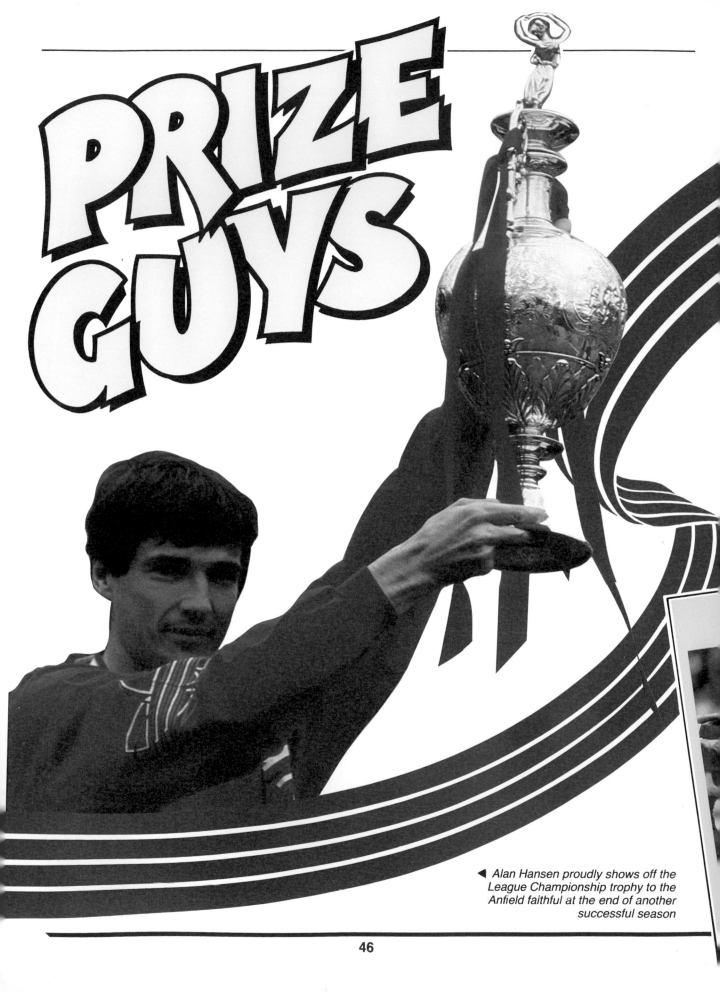

◄ Alan Hansen proudly shows off the
League Championship trophy to the
Anfield faithful at the end of another
successful season

LIVERPOOL

There are no prizes for guessing the name of the club which has stood out above all others in recent years. Last season they did it again, taking the championship with ease, and even though we did our best at Old Trafford to make sure it wasn't so simple, Liverpool stormed home.

Some critics have said that Liverpool's success is bad for the game, that the fact that they have had more than their fair share of trophies over the last 20 years has spoiled things. As far as I'm concerned that's rubbish.

Liverpool have set the standard we all have to achieve if we are to be successful.

Overdrive

Last season at Manchester United we had a campaign which in past years would definitely have taken the title, but Liverpool simply stepped up a gear, just like a top sprinter finding that bit extra when he is threatened in an Olympic final.

Over the last two decades they have demonstrated to other clubs that to be successful they have to overcome the might of Merseyside. If you think I'm exaggerating just check your record books. Even our two cup wins in 1977 and 1985 involved games against Liverpool, and when the prizes are dished out at the end of the season you can more or less guarantee that Liverpool will pick up something.

But what is the secret of Liverpool's success?

That's something people have been trying to put a finger on for years. A great system, a continuation of management, super fitness, fanatical support which is worth a goal start at home? All these theories have been tabled at some time or other, but to me the secret is far simpler than the reasons usually put forward . . . Liverpool's sides are made up of great players with the right attitude for success.

Team play

They have eleven men out on the pitch who can all read one another's game, and possess a tremendous amount of skill. They play for one another and that's the secret of any successful team.

Football's a team game and eleven skilled players working together as one unit will always win against a side made up of two or three individual stars and eight others there to make up the numbers.

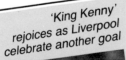
'King Kenny' rejoices as Liverpool celebrate another goal

If I was a little lad who supported Liverpool I think that the one picture on my bedroom wall which would be bigger than all the others would be one of Kenny Dalglish.

Kenny may well have more or less hung up his boots now, but he will always remain in my mind as a player of tremendous vision and skill. Men like Kevin Keegan were great, and Kevin's a smashing lad, but Kenny was special and his contribution to the success of Liverpool has been amazing. He was an extremely influential player and that is continuing now he is in charge.

47

Many people said that the Manchester United side of the sixties was a team of individuals, that George Best, Denis Law and Bobby Charlton were the main reasons for success. That simply wasn't true, any more than that John Barnes, Peter Beardsley and John Aldridge were mainly responsible for Liverpool's championship in 1988.

All-round strength

In the days of George Best United used around 20 players a season in their squad, and as well as the skills of Law, Best and Charlton up front they were pretty strong in other departments too.

That rule applies to Liverpool. Kenny Dalglish has been forced to use a variety of players during a season and still retained the form which took Liverpool to the top, but that is another reason why the club has been able to keep on winning.

It is very easy to introduce a fresh face to a side which is doing well. The confidence rubs off on the new player, and if he takes time to settle in the experience and the talent of those around him will carry him through.

It's a very different story plunging a young player into a side that's fighting off relegation. One mistake can mean disaster, and it's very easy to blame the new boy if something goes wrong in these circumstances.

Play from the back

I suppose that one of Liverpool's strengths over the years has been that they always play from the back.

At one time it was Emlyn Hughes and Phil Thompson who gave them solidarity, then Alan Hansen and Mark Lawrenson, and they all followed men like Ron Yeats and Tommy Smith.

Players like these could help develop the short passing game from the back four which has been Liverpool's trademark. If you are strong at the back that strength spreads through the side until you have a solid, effective outfit.

Long ball out

Some clubs have central defenders who can't dwell on the ball and have to get rid of it quickly, playing the long ball game, but that's not the Liverpool

The Red Machine steamrollers on with Everton's Dave Watson helpless to stop Peter Beardsley in a Mersey derby at Anfield

style. They play football right through the side.

One of the remarkable things about Liverpool has been that they have changed managers several times without there being any drop in performance. In fact it's fair to say that some of their greatest successes have come under Kenny Dalglish and he did little actually to build the club into the colossal institution it is today.

Kenny was a great player, but when he took over he was hardly being given charge of a side struggling to avoid relegation. He was given a firm foundation onto which he had to build his sides, and it is a much simpler job to do that than to start from scratch.

⚽ Shankly the great

The man who filled that role at Anfield was the great Bill Shankly. When he arrived at the club they had all sorts of problems, but when he retired the blueprint for success was drawn up – all his successors had to do was stick to the plans!

Even when the club has changed managers they have kept the continuity. Men have worked on under the new manager, for example Ronnie Moran is still there to assist Kenny, and that links today with years gone by. If Kenny wants any advice he can always turn to Ronnie, and of course Bob Paisley is there to help if necessary.

⚽ Kenny's problems

I think that Kenny must have had a difficult job at first when he became manager and suddenly found himself in charge of players he had shared rooms with, played alongside and trained with on the same level for years. That's changed, of course, as those players have moved on and he's been able to bring in his own selection.

Knowing Kenny, I reckon that he was shrewd enough to realise that one day he would become manager. I wouldn't mind betting that he had built up his own personal dossier of players he had faced and who he would like to have in his team in the future. That could be the secret

of the Liverpool side of 1988-89.

Whatever the reason for Liverpool's domination, it is anything but bad for the game. Liverpool are the trend-setters, the pace-makers, the champions and it's up to others to rise to their level . . . and who knows what lies beyond that?

◀ The Liverpool squad pose with their 17th Championship trophy

John Barnes, the brightest jewel in Liverpool's crown, worth all of the £900,000 Liverpool spent on bringing him to Anfield from Watford ▶

ROBBO'S QUIZ

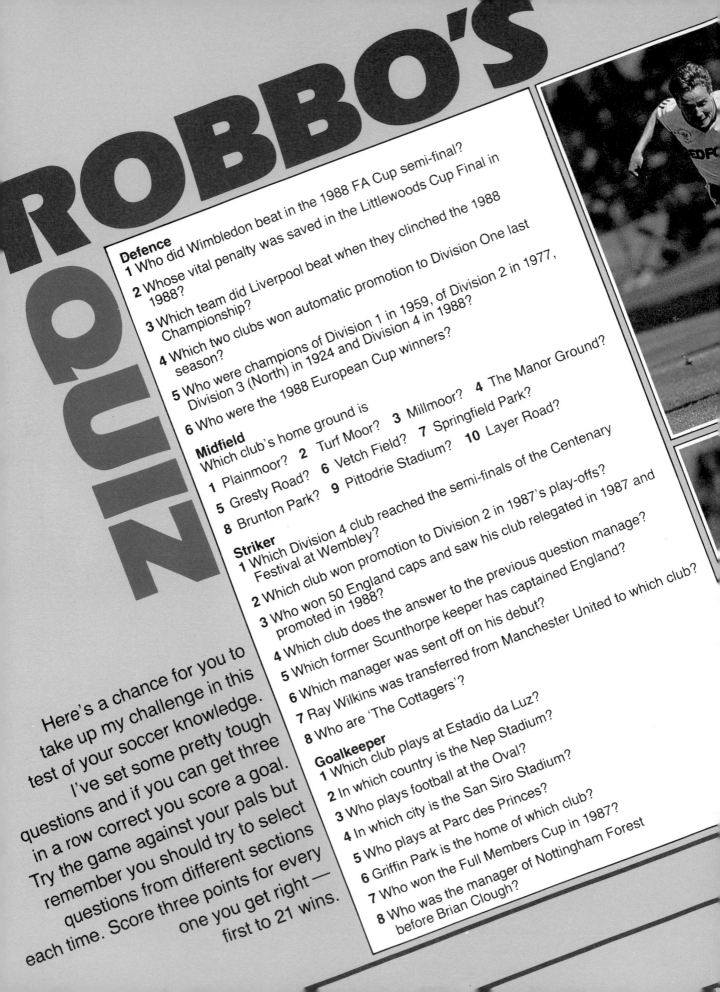

Defence

1 Who did Wimbledon beat in the 1988 FA Cup semi-final?
2 Whose vital penalty was saved in the Littlewoods Cup Final in 1988?
3 Which team did Liverpool beat when they clinched the 1988 Championship?
4 Which two clubs won automatic promotion to Division One last season?
5 Who were champions of Division 1 in 1959, of Division 2 in 1977, Division 3 (North) in 1924 and Division 4 in 1988?
6 Who were the 1988 European Cup winners?

Midfield

Which club's home ground is
1 Plainmoor? 2 Turf Moor? 3 Millmoor? 4 The Manor Ground?
5 Gresty Road? 6 Vetch Field? 7 Springfield Park?
8 Brunton Park? 9 Pittodrie Stadium? 10 Layer Road?

Striker

1 Which Division 4 club reached the semi-finals of the Centenary Festival at Wembley?
2 Which club won promotion to Division 2 in 1987's play-offs?
3 Who won 50 England caps and saw his club relegated in 1987 and promoted in 1988?
4 Which club does the answer to the previous question manage?
5 Which former Scunthorpe keeper has captained England?
6 Which manager was sent off on his debut?
7 Ray Wilkins was transferred from Manchester United to which club?
8 Who are 'The Cottagers'?

Goalkeeper

1 Which club plays at Estadio da Luz?
2 In which country is the Nep Stadium?
3 Who plays football at the Oval?
4 In which city is the San Siro Stadium?
5 Who plays at Parc des Princes?
6 Griffin Park is the home of which club?
7 Who won the Full Members Cup in 1987?
8 Who was the manager of Nottingham Forest before Brian Clough?

Here's a chance for you to take up my challenge in this test of your soccer knowledge. I've set some pretty tough questions and if you can get three in a row correct you score a goal. Try the game against your pals but remember you should try to select questions from different sections each time. Score three points for every one you get right — first to 21 wins.

Try this game with your pals.

If you get two in a row correct, ask him a goalkeeper question, if he gets it right he makes a save, if not you have scored without answering a third question. Vary the game to make it more fun, one question each and give away a goal when you slip up.

◀ANSWERS

Training for an international. Physical fitness and tactical coaching needs work more than technique

ENGLAND

Playing for your country is a great thrill, but it can also be a lot of fun. For me there is nothing like an England get-together – and that isn't meant to be any reflection on my colleagues at Old Trafford – but meeting up with players from other clubs is always interesting.

Over the years that I've played for England I've come into close contact with many lads from every possible part of the country, and when we exchange stories about life at our various clubs, about how different coaches approach training, tactics and such like, it all adds to the pleasure I get out of football.

We meet the quiet types, the thinkers, the readers, the jokers – just about every contrast you would get in any walk of life,

BEHIND THE SCENES

although the fact that we are all footballers gives us one thing in common – a love of the game.

Wembley warm-ups

The normal routine for a Wembley game is for us to report to the England headquarters on Sunday night, having played for our clubs on the Saturday.

The Boss – Bobby Robson – gets us all together for a team talk in which he tells us his plans for the build-up to the game. He lays out his plan of action, tells us when we'll be training and so on, and when that's all over it's time for a meal and then off to bed.

Monday morning means a full training session with a variety of exercises, and plenty of hard work. Then in the afternoon we usually have free time, when some of us go off to the local cinema, which is one of those multi-screen places, and others pop down the road for a game of snooker.

Everybody gets back to headquarters for 7 pm when it's down to the business of eating and sleeping once more before training again the day before the game.

I suppose it would be very easy to get bored, but after a hard session on the field the relaxation helps build up the energy for the next day.

Like every club side, England has its share of jokers and for the last few years Kenny Sansom of Arsenal has been the life and soul of the party. He's got a great repertoire of impersonations, including Michael Crawford, Prince Charles and such like, and he never stops wisecracking.

Playing abroad

When we're playing abroad it's lads like Kenny who help to keep us in a good mood. He's always ready for a laugh and it's smashing to be in his company.

The problem with away games

"For about seven years I shared a room with Ray Wilkins whenever we were both in the England squad, but since Ray lost his place I've been paired with Gary Mabbutt and Viv Anderson. Both are great lads and Viv is a bundle of energy. I think he spends all day and evening talking, but when he gets back to the room he just collapses on his bed and goes to sleep, so that suits me!"

is usually that there aren't the facilities for relaxation that there are at home and as we usually spend a longer time on foreign trips, we have to make sure that we take plenty of video tapes, lots of music cassettes and plenty to read with us.

Then there are the card schools, of course, and I've got to confess that I'm a member of one of these, along with players like Peter Shilton, Tony Cottee (when he's in the squad), Kenny Sansom and Chris Woods, and that takes up a lot of spare time.

Glenn Hoddle's our music man, and he will always turn up with a tape recorder and a pile of cassettes, so there's never a dull moment even when we are away from home for a long spell such as for the World Cup or the European Championships.

But whoever is in the squad and wherever we are it's always an enjoyable time and something we will never forget. Playing for your country is a great honour, being in the England squad is tremendous fun, and I've loved every minute of it.

Teamwork is vital in internationals, so there is greater emphasis on set-pieces and playing together in training
▼

THE DREAM TEAM –

If you could select a side to play against any other, anywhere in the world, who would it include? That was the question the editor asked me as we planned this section of the annual, and I can assure you it was no easy task.

Now I know how Bobby Robson feels when he says it was a difficult decision about who to choose for an England game, or why we see so many variations of possible line-ups on the sports pages before squads are named for competitions like the World Cup or the European Championship.

However, the "Robson World Eleven" is all my own work and there are no outside influences. I didn't even tell the lads at Old Trafford what I was doing when they saw me sitting in the corner of the dressing-room after training, scribbling names down in my diary.

The rules I had to stick to were to select players who were still in the game and who I would like to play alongside.

I know there are a few surprises, but here's who I've chosen as the ten men in my team, with my reasons.

Peter Shilton What can I say about Peter that hasn't been said already? He has been the best goalkeeper in the world for the last seven or eight years and I've chosen him despite the fact that there are some younger keepers coming through to challenge. Experience is a great asset to a goalkeeper and Peter has plenty of that. If a young player wants to model himself on a top professional he need not look any further than Shilts for a great example of how hard work and dedication will lead to success.

Manuel Amaros The Frenchman with the Spanish name is my chosen right full-back. What a player he is — a solid defender, a good reader of the game and fast

PETER SHILTON

MANUEL AMAROS

JOSE LUIS BROWN

MY WORLD ELEVEN

and strong in the tackle. These are essentials in a full-back, but he is also very good going forward and can add that extra dimension to your side, overlapping with the wide mid-field men.

Jose Luis Brown He is the first of my two central defenders. He's the mainstay of the Argentinian defence and what I call an out-and-out attacker of the ball. By that I mean he wants it whenever it is within his reach. The world saw how good Jose is at getting into scoring positions when he grabbed that vital goal in the 1986 World Cup final and that's the sort of thing I'd expect from him in my team. (If only he had been just plain Joe Brown of England!)

Glenn Heysen The tall blond Swede is extremely good in the air and can play sweeper as well as central defender, which I think is the role that I would want him to fill. Like Brown he is very good at set-pieces and gets into scoring positions, which is one of the strengths of a good side. It isn't only the strikers who score goals, but the big men at the back. He was linked with Manchester United in 1987 but chose Italian football instead.

Antonio Cabrini This Italian may just be coming to the end of his international career, but I would want him in my side to give it experience as well as a strong left-back. Cabrini has been at the top for a long time and I bet that you can count the number of goals he has given away on one hand! Like Amaros on the other side, he is fast, solid and a quick thinker who gets himself out of trouble by being in the right place at the right time.

Salvatore Bagni The Italian midfielder gets through so much hard work that he has earned his place ahead of many others. He is a good ball winner and when he has got it you can't get it off him again, unless you are on his side. Then he keeps the passing simple and

SALVATORE BAGNI

ANTONIO CABRINI

GLENN HEYSEN

I knew that I couldn't pick a World Eleven without Ruud Gullit and Diego Maradona, so I wrote their names down first, then my keeper, and worked my way through the side like that. Now all I'd like to do is get them together for a game!

RUUD GULLIT

GHEORGHE HAGI

THE DREAM TEAM –

he fills the role of the defensive mid-field player perfectly.

Ruud Gullit He would be my other partner in mid-field and although I could have named him as one of my strikers I think the big Dutchman would be better making those surging runs of his from deeper positions. What havoc he could create with accurate passes to the front men. I also think it would be a great thrill to play alongside Bagni and Gullit. I'm sure we would all enjoy it.

Gheorghe Hagi You may not know a lot about this Romanian midfielder, but having played against him twice and seen him in action for Steaua Bucharest I know that I would like him in my World Eleven. He is the top man in Romanian soccer and he's been a full international since he was 17, and you must be good to have credentials like that. He'd play on my left side and I'd expect a lot of goals from him.

Diego Maradona There is no way I could leave him out – if I'm supposed to be picking the best, Diego's got to be there. Every time he goes onto a football pitch he can either score or create a goal and that is the hardest thing to do, but he makes it look easy. He has great vision and has so many tricks up his sleeve you wonder what he will try next.

Emilio Butragueno He is my other striker and this was my hardest choice. I found myself with half a dozen I would have liked in the side, but I had to make a choice and I think that Emilio would be the best alongside Maradona. My others included Hugo Sanchez and Gary Lineker, but I've decided on Butragueno because he's such an instinctive goal-scorer, just like his partner up front. He's brilliant when he has his back to the goal and has to turn and score. That's when he is at his most dangerous.

So there you have it, the results of my hard work. I don't expect you to agree with my selection, but it's my team and nobody else's.

I realise that apart from me — and the rules said I had to play — there is only one British player in

DIEGO MARADONA

EMILIO BUTRAGUENO

MY WORLD ELEVEN

the side. That is not intended to be a reflection on any of my England pals, or in any way is it meant to be critical of our domestic players. I have picked those I think are the best in the whole of football.

Now you select your side, fix up a venue and we'll give you a game . . . and that I suppose is where I wake up, because trying to get all ten players together at the same time would be a much harder job than selecting the team.

		SHILTON (England)		
AMAROS (France)	BROWN (Argentina)	HEYSEN (Sweden)	CABRINI (Italy)
BAGNI (Italy)	ROBSON (England)	GULLIT (Holland)	HAGI (Romania)
	MARADONA (Argentina)		BUTRAGUENO (Spain)

Now who wants to be an international manager!

Here's a tricky question for you. Name the man who in recent years has probably made the biggest impact on British soccer, the person who has done something which could influence the future development of the game and really put us back on the soccer map?

The answer will stun you.

As far as I'm concerned the man who fills this role is Nigel Lawson, Chancellor of the Exchequer!

It may seem hard to swallow and there may be one or two raised eyebrows, but I honestly believe that when the government decided to cut the highest rate of income tax to 40 pence in the pound in the spring of 1988, it did a tremendous job for football.

⚽ It's a short life

For years our top managers have struggled to keep the stars in Britain, but the lure of the lira, the persuasion of the peseta and the draw of the Deutschmark have attracted our stars. Who could blame them for going?

A player's career is very short. We may get paid attractive wages compared with people in ordinary jobs, but those wages stop once we get to our mid-30s, so in around 15 years we have to earn enough to keep us going for perhaps the rest of our lives. Foreign clubs offered financial security and tax rates in Italy, Spain and Germany meant that the taxman left you with a higher percentage of your pay than you could expect to take home in this country. Until 1988 that is.

Mr Lawson's tax adjustments meant that for every pound we earned we could keep 60 pence and for

Robson for Italy!

There was a time when it looked as if I would go abroad. All the top players were playing in Italy and it looked as if that was where I would finish up. I felt that it would be a great challenge to play alongside and against men like Maradona and Platini and the Brazilians, but when United asked for £3 million, which was much more than AC Milan had said they would offer, that was the end of that.

I was given the chance to sign a seven-year contract and was quite happy to stay in this country – even if the tax rate was higher then!

THE LURE O

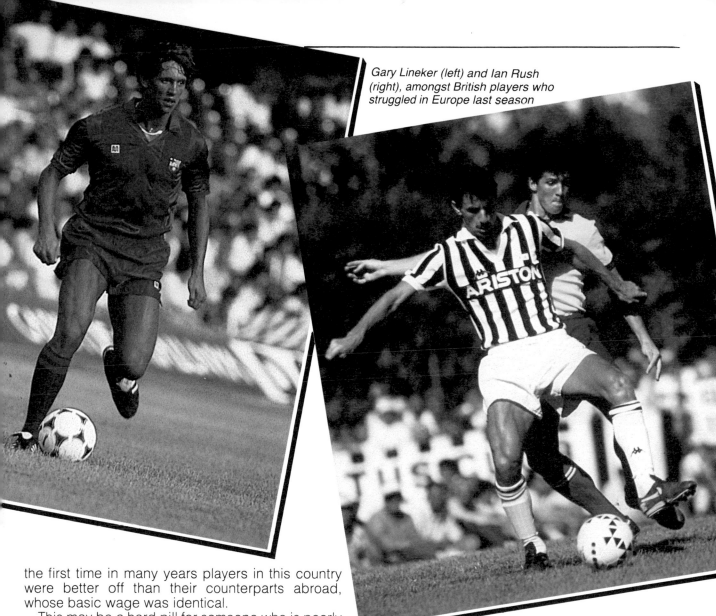

Gary Lineker (left) and Ian Rush (right), amongst British players who struggled in Europe last season

the first time in many years players in this country were better off than their counterparts abroad, whose basic wage was identical.

This may be a hard pill for someone who is poorly paid or out of work to swallow, but if it helps to keep their favourite players in this country I hope they'll see it from our point of view.

 Stop the exodus

I'm sure that players will think twice before going abroad because they keep 60 per cent rather than the 40 per cent they took home before the Budget and I'm sure players will stay here now, strengthening our game. Obviously there'll be exceptions: foreign clubs will wave fat cheques and this may persuade some to take the gamble, but I think that the recent records of our players abroad will also stop the talent exodus.

Some have hit it off overseas, Kevin Keegan in Germany for example, but the list of those who've been reported to be unsettled is lengthy and they've found out that European fans are far more fickle than ours! I can even see more foreign players coming to this country because of our reduced taxation, and that'll be another boost for the game.

So that's why Mr Lawson did his bit for football when he opened his battered Budget box in 1988 and it could have a long lasting effect on our game.

F THE LIRA

1994 ~WORLD CUP

The Best Ever!

One of my biggest regrets is that I'm going to miss what could be the best World Cup there's ever been, when the Yanks stage the 1994 finals.

Don't get me wrong. I'm sure the Italians will do their best in 1990, and that all the stops were pulled out in 1966 when it was our turn, but when the Americans get their hands on anything it usually turns out to be bigger and better than ever before!

Scoreboard in America. As American grounds often stage more than one sport they have to give more information than just the score ▼

Communications

The Americans have already shown the rest of the world what they can do when it comes to organising spectacular events in boxing, golf and tennis, and after the Olympic Games there is only one major sporting event which remains unexplored for them, and that is the World Cup.

The hotels, the facilities available for players, officials, the media and spectators will be second to none, and communications will be fantastic.

I'm sure that the pitches will be perfect as well. The only problem there will be as far as I can see is that the distances between group bases could be further than ever before. That might just cause a few problems for the teams taking part if they're jumping on and off aircraft every couple of days.

 ## The game in America

I think the one thing which is going to make the event a world-wide success will be that the Americans will be competing themselves, and if they can get into the quarter-finals, or even further, the crowds are going to flock to the matches.

Soccer in America is developing fast. I know that the game doesn't seem to have the same draw on our players that it did five or six years ago, but what is happening now is that the kids who took up the sport as teenagers, or ten-year-olds, are starting to emerge and they'll be the boys who make the American World Cup squad of 1994.

Schools and colleges are playing soccer in America and there's no doubting that the 16-year-olds of today are going to figure strongly in the World Cup planning.

They'll also have a place for players who've settled in the States from football-playing nations and I wouldn't be surprised to see them doing better than most people would expect.

By 1994 technology will have advanced beyond today's limits and who knows what America will hold in store for the football fan five years from now? When Jules Rimet first had the idea of a World Cup there was no television, when England won in 1966 viewers watched in black and white, so who knows what 1994 might have in store for us?

Will we watch the matches in hologram form projected onto a table-top soccer pitch? Or will it be flat screen television sets hanging on the wall of our homes with stereo sound making us feel part of the American version of the Mexican wave? Whatever it is, you can guarantee that the World Cup of 1994 will be something special. My only regret is that I won't be playing – but if anyone wants a commentator I'm available to offers!

The one major mistake the Americans made when they decided to launch soccer in their country a few years ago was to play around with the rules. They had penalty shoot-outs and such like and this made it impossible for them to join FIFA. That was a mistake. They are international soccer's governing body and if you don't step into line with them then you are obviously going to be left out of competitions. Americans love their sports and that's why I think that it's essential that a US team does well in 1994, and that could pave the way for a great development of the sport in the States in the future.

The Aztec Stadium, Mexico City, has staged two World Cup Finals ▶

◀ *Tampa Bay Rowdies cheerleaders (the Wowdies) give their team moral support. Would they still smile if it was snowing?*